D1389320

The Little
Book of
Witchcraft

This book is dedicated to Noelle and Elizabeth, my coven, for their invaluable help and support.

The Little
Book of
Witchcraft

Kitty Guilsborough

An Hachette UK Company
www.hachette.co.uk

First published in Great Britain in 2019 by Gaia Books,
an imprint of Octopus Publishing Group Ltd
Carmelite House
50 Victoria Embankment
London EC4Y 0DZ
www.octopusbooks.co.uk

Distributed in the US by Hachette Book Group,
1290 Avenue of the Americas, 4th and 5th Floors, New York, NY 10104

Distributed in Canada by Canadian Manda Group,
664 Annette Street, Toronto, Ontario, Canada M6S 2C8

ISBN 978-1-85675-395-1

A CIP catalogue record for this book is available from the British Library.

Printed and bound in China.

10 9 8 7 6 5 4 3 2 1

Publishing Director: Stephanie Jackson
Art Director: Juliette Norsworthy
Junior Editor: Sarah Vaughan
Designer and Illustrator: Abi Read
Copy Editor: Clare Churly
Production Controller: Allison Gonsalves

Contents

Introduction

This book is a practical introduction to witchcraft for busy women with ordinary lives.

Now, look, I know that maybe you're sceptical: the word "witchcraft" carries an awful lot of cultural weight, after all, and most of it isn't good. You're thinking of pointy hats, Harry Potter and warts. You're thinking of toads and the moon. And honestly? There's nothing wrong with toads or Harry Potter. Warts can be both treated and/or beautiful. Pointy hats are a style choice. And this was never going to be the kind of book where we speak ill of the moon. But witchcraft is so much more than these things – and if you let it, it will change your life.

Why Witchcraft?

So much of what we call "witchcraft" is really the art of listening to yourself and others, picking up on vibes and feelings and the subtle things that happen all around you. In some ways, witchcraft is simply applied mindfulness.

In this book we'll cover everything from a brief history of witches to creating your own witch's kit. There's a rough guide to crystals, a road map to Tarot, affirmations, incantations and (oh, let's just say it) spells for all kinds of occasion. There are herbs to grow, candles to make and burn, and meditations and visualizations on which to focus. There are exercises to help you tap into your feelings and most powerful truths, rituals to clarify your mind and traditions that will connect you to millennia of women who wanted (just like you) to take control of their lives.

I know what you're thinking. It's the big question: is it *really* magic?

I can't tell you whether or not to believe in magic. I can't even really tell you whether I do. But I can tell you that the study and practice of magic – along with the history, traditions, legends and rituals therein – can change your life for the better.

A Brief History of Witches

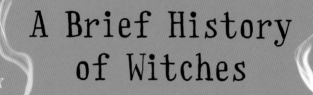

Witches have been part of human history for as long as women have existed, which is to say, forever. All through recorded history, alongside the bread and the beer, are witches. Occasionally societies honour them, more often than not they banish them, but they are always there. The history of witchcraft around the world is far too long for a little book like this, because it's really a history of rebellion and resilience in every country, in every society, at every time.

A Cultural Note

There are places in the world, still, where witchcraft is taken profoundly seriously. In Ghana, for example, "witch camps" are still in place for women – often widows – suspected of performing magic. There are numerous examples within the last ten years of places where spontaneous mobs have formed to attack and kill women suspected of performing magic. There are countries, such as Saudi Arabia, where witchcraft is not only illegal, but still, by law, punishable by death.

It's hard to know what to say about these terrible acts of violence, but it's important to take a moment to acknowledge them in a discussion of magic. It's essential to recognize that our practice of magic and spiritual self-help is intertwined fundamentally with an ongoing struggle that spans the globe.

Different countries have different kinds of magic, and different histories and stories of magic, and so often those stories come down to the oppression of women. To ignore that is to ignore a vital part of what has made witchcraft so powerful. It's crucial to acknowledge that much of magic is about the disputed right of women to think for themselves.

With that in mind, then, it's important to note that in this book we're talking chiefly about the witch in the West, where, whatever might be muttered in the pub, would-be witches can largely practise whatever kind of magic works best for them.

A History of Magic

A history of magic, whatever Harry Potter might have to say about it, could go on for thousands of pages, and needs a thousand experts to really get to grips with all the cultures, customs and ideas involved. After all, what's the exact definition of a "witch" – as opposed to a "sorceress" or a "hag" or an "enchantress"? Is a "witch" in English the same thing as a female practitioner of magic in any other language? It's hard to know.

Even the etymology of the word "witch" is difficult to pin down. It definitely derives from the Old English "wicca" or "wicce", which means pretty much the same thing. Where the word "wicce" comes from is harder to pin down; it might be from a word meaning "sacred", or from a word meaning "to make move", or from a word meaning "to wake" or "to speak" or "to know" or "to see". In other words, the term "witch" is as mysterious, vague and intriguing as the powers it encompasses.

It's this very vagueness that makes witchcraft so dangerous, and endangered. After all, when any woman can be powerful – in any of these different ways – she must be stopped. The history of witches in the Western world is largely a history of persecution. It isn't a nice story, but it's one that must be told in order to truly understand the nature of so many things about modern witchcraft.

Whatever private use people might have had for the wise woman in their village, the public, political position in the West has been against witchcraft for at least a thousand years. The Christian Bible exhorts for witches to be murdered (Exodus 22:18, if you want to look it up) and Pope Alexander IV sanctioned their executions in 1200.

Pope John XXII, in the mid-fourteenth century, explicitly condemned all witches and decreed that the full force of the law should be brought down upon them. Pope Innocent VIII, in 1484, doubled down on this in his *Summis desiderantes* – a papal bull regarding witchcraft – in which he called for witches to be "chastised ... according to their desserts". Mostly, these women were poor; they were oppressed, and sometimes outspoken. They were often ugly or old, or otherwise unavailable to men. Sometimes they had cats. Sometimes they read books. Sometimes they were clever. Were these women really "witches"? And what would it even mean if they were?

What matters to us, now, is that in our own practice we honour the memory of those women who wanted, for whatever reason, to live their own lives their own way. It matters that we use our practice of magic to live our lives *our* own way: the best way we can, and for the best reasons we can. We must use our practice of magic to connect with ourselves and with the world around us, and to do the most good we can.

Being Your Best Self

It's worth trying to live our lives as those persecuted witches might have done: by affirming our sense of self and our right to choose that self; by affirming our own path, and our right to choose that path; by affirming our own history, and our place in that history. This is all part of what a study of witchcraft helps us accomplish. We can belong to this tradition; we can belong to a sisterhood that extends through time; we can take up exactly as much space in the world as we need.

Can it feel silly to believe in magic? Of course.

Can it also feel silly, and perhaps dangerously self-indulgent, to believe in yourself? Absolutely.

These two things are intrinsically linked: allowing yourself to connect with your mind through candles, cards and crystals can help you to believe in other aspects of your life, too.

You don't have to start this book by believing in magic. You don't even have to start this book by believing in yourself. You simply have to want to.

Affirmations

Affirmations are designed to help you believe in yourself and in your right to assert what you want, what you have and what you need.

Each affirmation in this book follows a similar pattern: you'll light a candle, practise breathing and tune into your thoughts, feelings and sensations. The "affirmation" itself is a short statement you repeat (aloud if possible) that allows you to feel what it might be like to accept that statement as true.

Frequently, women are encouraged not to voice their own desires – or their own good qualities. We prize modesty, stoicism and putting other people first, and it's hard to break free of that cultural conditioning. Affirmations allow us a space to take back these perfectly ordinary ideas as our own. Saying something aloud allows us to break the taboo of the "secret thought", and while it might feel a little silly, it's actually based on sound psychological research. The ritual (the candle, the breathing, the chanting) gives us a framework for thinking about ourselves that somehow acts as permission to address these ideas.

Are these affirmations spells? Sort of, I suppose. They employ the trappings of magic to give us permission to use our own strength, our own decisions and our own self-confidence for whatever we need.

A Brief History of Witches

EXERCISE:
Affirmation of Self

We'll start with an exercise designed to affirm and
acknowledge your self, and the path you are on. It also
affirms your right, if you want, to use ritual, history,
superstition, lore and (yes!) magic to help you get where you
want to be. Repeat this affirmation daily for best effects.

You will need: a candle.

1 Light the candle and sit comfortably facing the flame.
   For about two minutes, focus on the flame, looking at
   each part of it. Really concentrate on the flame: the pale
   yellow, the deeper orange, the small triangle of bright blue
   around the wick. This will feel like a long time to focus
   on one thing, but stick with it.

2 Take that concentration and apply it to your own breath.
   Notice how your breath fills your chest, your lungs and,
   perhaps, if you're breathing deeply, your diaphragm and
   belly, too. Notice how your shoulders rise and fall with
   your breath. Notice how the breath feels in your throat.

3 Now, we're going to try to even out that breath. Do
   whatever feels comfortable to you, but I'd recommend

breathing in for six counts, holding your breath for seven, and releasing your breath for eight. Give yourself three or four minutes to try to get this breath even. Really focus on the way it feels, keeping your eyes fixed on the candle.

4 When you feel that your breath is even and steady, it's time to begin the affirmation. Say aloud, repeating each line five times:

I matter.

I matter, and my ideas matter.

I matter, and my opinions matter.

I matter, and my decisions matter.

I matter.

5 Bring your focus back to your breath, and then, slowly, back to the candle. How do you feel?

Whether saying this affirmation has changed your view of yourself or not (and I'm willing to bet that doing it once hasn't made much difference!), the ritualized chanting, the candle and the breathwork create an altered state of consciousness: one where you're ready to begin the serious practices of both magic and self-knowledge.

What Makes a Witch?

Magic is sometimes defined as "that which connects", and this chapter is all about the different ways we can start to connect with magic itself. Now, look, I've said already that you don't have to believe in magic for this book to be helpful to you.

What you do need, however, is an open mind and a sense that nobody has all the answers. You need a readiness to connect with the world, with yourself and with the people and beings all around you, and a sense that you are capable of doing so. This is all it takes to be a witch.

Some people might disagree. Some people would prefer witchcraft to be an elite club with initiations and secrets that belong to a chosen few. This is, quite simply, ridiculous: it's transposing the trappings of a difficult, highly engineered world onto something wild and beautiful and free. We are all equal here. Your magic is as valuable and important as mine. You are as valuable and important as I am. You are, for the intents and purposes of this book, a witch now. Welcome.

For whatever reason, you've been drawn to witchcraft (or someone who loves you thinks it might suit you). Maybe this is because you believe in the supernatural. Maybe this is because you believe that there are forces beyond our control. Maybe you don't know what you believe. Maybe you just wear a lot of black. (Hi, friend!)

In any case, you're here. In the previous pages, we've discussed witchcraft around the world and through time, and asserted our own right to choose, as well as our right to have whatever ideas we want. We've legitimized witchcraft with a history; positioned it in a global and political context; and given a sensible, everyday reason for doing it in the first place: to connect with ourselves and with the world around us, and to live up to the potential within.

So how do we do that? It's time to think practically about how witchcraft can form part of our lives, and what that might look like.

The Different Kinds of Witches

London-based witch and writer Caroline O'Donoghue once said that there are three main kinds of witch: what she laughingly calls "story witches, ritual witches and stuff witches".

"Story witches," she explains, "are into folklore and Tarot and symbols. They like talking things out and generally just weaving the whole thing with words."

"Ritual witches like *doing* stuff. Chanting, planning, growing, lighting things on fires, etc. [They're sort of the] 'proactive gardener' kind of witches."

And stuff witches? "Stuff witches," O'Donoghue says, "find a lot of strength in "things", such as carrying a really good stone. They might have an altar in their home."

Of course, most of us can identify a little with all three of these categories; they aren't mutually exclusive. But you probably find yourself drawn to one of these categories. For example, I'm mostly a story witch, but with a side order of stuff witch: I practise Tarot, but have a really good stone tucked into the pocket of most of my coats. This doesn't mean I don't ever use ritual – I light a candle to help focus good thoughts, for example – but it's not exactly my go-to mode.

I have a friend who is mostly a ritual witch: she does real spells, lights coloured candles and burns various herbs. Sometimes she is interested in symbols, but only if they relate

to her rituals. She's interested in stuff, but only insofar as it's useful to her in her thoughtful, considered spellcraft.

Different witches use different tools and techniques to connect with the universe and with themselves (and you'd be surprised at how often that amounts to exactly the same thing). Over the next few chapters, we'll look at some of those tools and techniques in detail. You might already know what kind of thing you're interested in. Or, perhaps, you're starting from the very beginning. The quiz on the following pages will help you work out which kind of witch you might be. But remember, the quiz doesn't define you, or your magic; it's simply a guide to help you get to where you want to be.

Which Witch Are You?

Read each question and circle the option that is most like you.

YOUR FRIEND IS IN CRISIS! YOU...

A Bring over a casserole.

B Talk it out.

C Send flowers, so they know you're thinking of them.

YOU'VE GOT A FREE SATURDAY! YOU GO TO A...

A Farmer's market.

B Library.

C Junk shop.

YOU'RE PICKING A NEW HOBBY! YOU CHOOSE...

A Archery.

B Creative writing.

C Pottery.

YOU'RE TROUBLED BY POLITICS! YOU...

A Go out and protest!

B Design, sign and circulate a petition.

C Get busy making, selling and buying handicrafts
in aid of the Revolution.

YOU'VE WON THE LOTTERY! YOU IMMEDIATELY...

A Hire an accountant and a lawyer and set up a
foundation for charitable causes.

B Start looking through the stories of everyone who
won the lottery before you; become panicked that
the money is cursed; and ask everyone you know
how best to spend it.

C Pay off your debts, buy your mother a house and
buy yourself a truly magnificent gown for more
money than you've ever spent in your life.

If you chose mostly As: You're probably
a ritual witch. You like doing things. You're
practical. You want to make a tisane while
thinking careful, orderly thoughts. You want
to garden. You're interested in making stuff
happen. You're a hands-on kind of witch. You'll
probably be into candles, incantations and small
practical magics to make things better.

If you chose mostly Bs:
You might be a story witch. You
like knowing the history of things.
You like being part of a great tradition.
You like ideas, and words, and
overthinking. You talk about all of your
feelings, and you mostly feel better
afterward. You'll probably get a kick out
of Tarot, the moon and keeping a journal.

If you chose mostly Cs: You could be a stuff witch.
You're into being able to see the fruits of your labours,
and you surround yourself with them.
You're a fabulous gift-giver. You know
exactly what you like. You may hate
to throw things away. You'll probably
enjoy using crystals, candles and
keeping a journal.

Making Time

What do I mean when I talk about "making time"?
Well, you don't need to rush to your nearest witch shop for supplies, although it's true they're always worth a wander around if you're into incense, crystals or tiny figurines of fairies (and who isn't?). All you need in the first instance is to allocate a little bit of time to yourself. It could be half an hour, an hour or maybe even an entire evening when you're not doing anything and everybody else is out.

You might feel, instantly, that this is impossible. How could you make that time? You've got a million demands on you. You're busy every night this week. And when you're home, you're going to have to think about laundry and the freezer and whether you sent that email. You're just going to shove this book in your bag and read it on the bus, and that will be fine.

Well, that will be fine, as far as it goes. Will it change your life? Probably not. Will it, in fact, change anything? Probably not. Does something need to change? Well, if you haven't got a single evening when you can sit down and have a think about your life, goals, needs, wants and desires, it feels like something might need to change.

Just like mindfulness and other kinds of meditation, much of witchcraft is about simply taking the time to listen to yourself and to the world around you. Listening and paying attention are much of what keeps us all grounded and sane. If your life has become so hectic, so stressful and so busy that you don't have that time, it's no wonder that you sometimes feel like things are out of your control. It's no wonder that you've started wondering whether there's another way.

There is another way – and here we are. Using your results from the quiz on the previous pages as a guide, have a quick look at the activities outlined under each quiz result and see if any of those things grab you. As you progress, you might want to buy a deck of Tarot cards or some relevant crystals; you might want to plant-up a window box or organize a monthly spell night with like-minded friends. You might want to buy candle-making supplies or other craft bits and bobs. You might want nothing: you might be the kind of witch who finds power simply in meditating on a single flame, or in the in and out of her own breath. There are many different ways to be a witch, and each of those ways is as valid and meaningful as any other. Each of those ways is powerful, and each of those ways relies on your taking a little time to notice yourself, the people around you and the world you live in.

What Makes a Witch?

So what makes a witch? Well, it's the willingness to try and the willingness to affirm the power within. You are, believe it or not, extremely powerful. You can do anything you set your mind to. Practising magic (probably) won't make you madly wealthy; it won't solve everything in your life. What it can and will do is clarify your thoughts and feelings – and help you to turn those thoughts and feelings into action.

You have the power to change. You have the power to succeed. The affirmation on the following pages is an affirmation of your own power.

EXERCISE:

Affirmation of Power and Self

Before you start, you need to take some time to think about things you value about yourself and make a list of positive attributes about your personality. Maybe you can think of things people have said about you that made you feel valued and special; maybe you are secretly proud of how thoughtful you are, or how well you play the piano, or how often you listen when your loved ones need to be heard. Take a few moments to jot these things down – you'll need them in step 2 of this exercise.

You will need: a candle – a gold candle can feel particularly powerful. If you like, you can turn this affirmation into a "spell" with a small piece of rose quartz, a small square of cloth (big enough to completely contain the crystal) and a ribbon. This will allow you to make a little token of your own strength as a reminder of your own power and self-esteem. It's lovely, but not completely necessary.

1 Light the candle. Focus for a moment on the flame,
   then turn that attention to your breath.

2 With the rose quartz in your hand, if using, say:

   *My name is [your name]; I am [a positive attribute from your
   prepared list – for example, "I am kind"].*

   Repeat this formula with all the positive attributes on
   your list – everything you value about yourself and all the
   reasons that you are a strong, brave, brilliant person.

3 Then, still with the rose quartz in your hand, if using, and
   your eyes on the flame, say:

   My name is [your name], and I am powerful.

   My name is [your name], and I am capable.

   My name is [your name], and I am strong.

   *These are the reasons I love myself; and these are the reasons
   I'm worthy of love.*

4 If you're using the rose quartz, wrap it in the cloth and tie the top tightly with the ribbon, repeating three times:

This is a token of my strength; this is a token of my power.

I am worthy of love.

Keep the token with you as a reminder of how good you are. You are good. You matter. You're worthwhile and you're brilliant and you're brave.

The Four Elements

Traditionally, there are four elements: Earth, Air, Water and Fire. Sometimes these elements are associated with star signs (a Pisces, for example, is a Water sign) or the cardinal direction (East is Air; South is Fire; West is Water; and North is Earth) or colours, or personality traits or planets.

The four elements are often used in "sympathetic magic", whereby a physical object (or representative of the elements) is used to symbolize something wider. Commonly, the four elements are honoured at the start of a spell. Some witches begin rituals by calling upon and thanking each element. Some are sure to have a representative of each element in their spells and homes. And others believe that it's the balance of these four elements that makes the universe work.

You don't have to be a witch, however, to realize that this sense of balance can be useful to us in our own lives. To hold these four elements happily in tandem – each complemented by the others – is crucial for every one of us.

We use the four elements in both a practical and symbolic sense, then, to learn balance and acceptance. On the following pages, we'll do a quick assessment of where these elements turn up in their most practical sense in your life.

Finding the Elements

The first and most essential purpose of acknowledging the elements is a very practical nod to self-care. This exercise is designed to make you think about specific moments in your life when you took the time to notice the world around you. It encourages you to reflect on those moments of power and beauty and acknowledge the extraordinary energy of everything. This kind of gratitude and connection to the world can have a profound effect on your happiness, and your success.

You will need: a pen and paper.

1 Ask yourself the questions on the opposite page.

2 Take a moment now to jot down a time that you remember engaging properly and profoundly with each element. Perhaps you've recently been wild swimming or taken a blissfully hot bath – the element of Water. Perhaps you've chopped a handful of fresh herbs or buried your nose in a blooming rose – Earth. Perhaps you've watched a gull wheeling through the sky or flown a kite – Air. Or perhaps you've built a bonfire or lit a candle for a special occasion – Fire. These examples all count as honouring the elements!

DO I HAVE ALL FOUR ELEMENTS IN MY LIFE?

ARE THEY IN BALANCE?

AM I ALLOWING THESE FOUR ELEMENTS OF MY
LIFE TO BLOSSOM?

AM I GROUNDING MYSELF IN THE WORLD,
BUT STILL ALLOWING MYSELF TIME TO DREAM
WITH MY HEAD IN THE CLOUDS?

A Sense of Balance

You don't have to be a witch to be grateful for a refreshing breeze; or the solid earth beneath your feet; or a cool drink of water on a summer's day; or a roaring fire on a cold night. All four elements are necessary: the cool drink of water wouldn't be so beautiful without the fiery heat of the sun. No element is better than the others; no element can exist alone.

This sense of balance (of give-and-take) can help us to acknowledge our own emotions and the validity of our feelings. For example, just as Fire has a place in the four elements, so too does anger have a necessary place in our lives. Furthermore, just as a fire can be a terrifying conflagration or a comforting little blaze in the hearth, so our emotions come in many forms, shifting and changing over the course of our lives. And all of this is perfectly natural.

The Fifth Element

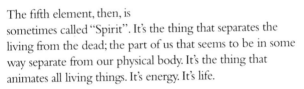

A fifth element? Yes, I told you
there were only four elements, and
that's true, in a purely physical
sense, but it's impossible to speak
of magic, witchcraft and
self-care without speaking
of the fifth element, too.

The fifth element, then, is
sometimes called "Spirit". It's the thing that separates the
living from the dead; the part of us that seems to be in some
way separate from our physical body. It's the thing that
animates all living things. It's energy. It's life.

We must acknowledge and honour this life force. We must
acknowledge its presence within us, just as we acknowledge
the Water in our blood, the Fire in the sun that warms us
and the Air we breathe. We must acknowledge the spark of
life that animates us; that gives power to our choices and
somehow, simultaneously, separates and unites us with the
world. The fact of our lives is a miracle; the fact that we all
are here is a miracle, and it's this that we acknowledge in the
next exercise.

Honouring the Elements

This exercise makes an excellent starting point for meditation, spellcasting, Tarot or magic in general.

You will need: five candles.

1 Arrange the candles on a table like this: one in the north, to represent Earth; one in the south, for Fire; one in the west, for Water; one in the east, for Air; and one in the centre, for Spirit.

2 Focus on the central candle and the clearest, brightest, whitest part of the flame. Visualize that white light moving outward, in a widening circle, encompassing the four remaining candles and absorbing their white light. Gradually visualize this light filling the room.

3 Within your circle of light, focus for a moment on each candle and the element it represents. Think of a time when Water seemed most pure; Fire most bright; Air most clean; and the Earth most solid, stable and full of potential to nourish. Focus on these moments for each flame and then welcome each element (either silently or out loud) into your life.

The Four Elements

Crystals for Beginners

It's easy to feel that these beautiful stones contain something special. Of course, you don't *need* crystals to practise meditation, mindfulness and concentrated attention; a stone from a park could do the same job, if it holds your focus, but it wouldn't be nearly as beautiful.

The science of crystals, and in particular crystal healing, is controversial and much debated. Luckily, that isn't our problem: we don't have to worry about *why* crystals work, as long as we can make them work for us. This book is all about using the tools of witchcraft to make the lives of busy, modern people easier – not about digging down into whether magic is real. You believe, or you don't. You're willing to try, or you're not. It's as simple as that.

So leave your scepticism at the door. Allow yourself to enter a world of shimmering colours and lights, and discover a very real connection with the Earth.

How Do Crystals Work?

Over the years, people have attributed all kinds of powers to crystals. In modern parlance, though, it's often said that crystals "vibrate" at different frequencies, giving each stone a different energy. There's some scientific truth to this, but for our purposes, what matters is the way that crystals give you a solid connection to the world around you and a tangible focus for your energies.

You can't look at a crystal and not feel a little awe and gratitude to live in a world where such things exist – and gratitude has a profound effect on our brains. Being consciously grateful for things can make a huge difference to depression and anxiety, and it can lift our moods, too. Having a token of our gratitude to the Earth and for our existence can only help us.

It's said that different kinds of stone have different properties, and that crystals with different shapes have different properties, too. Is this true? Well, it's scientifically documented that certain colours can become associated in our minds with particular emotions; and we know that different patterns of light can have interesting and profound effects on the brain. For example, a highly polished heart-shaped rose quartz is bound to make us think of

romance, and that,
in turn, helps us
to focus our
energies on what
we might want
from romance, or what
we might need from it, or
what we might hope for.

As with a candle flame, crystals are a locus for meditation: a centre of our energy and power. There's a power in owning something beautiful that's just for you, or choosing the right symbol for a friend. There is a power in owning exactly the right token for the person you want to be. I wear a labradorite necklace, for instance, as part of my quest to become more aware of what's magic in the world around me; and a pyramid-shaped chunk of peacock ore (or bornite) sits on my bookshelf to remind me that happiness is always possible. Is there some inherent magical quality in these stones that makes a difference? Or are they significant because thoughtful friends picked them out for me and I get to look at tangible and present reminders of my friends' love, my aspirations and how lucky I've been? Does it even matter which?

Choosing Your Crystals

When purchasing crystals, it's often worth asking the shop's proprietor for advice, but if you'd prefer to do your crystal shopping alone, here's a quick guide to help you select your crystals.

Crystals and Their Properties

Citrine: sunshine

Amethyst: stress relief

Rose Quartz: love

Clear Quartz: clarity

Labradorite: curiosity

Tiger's Eye: perspective

Malachite: transformation

Turquoise: protection

Shapes and Their Properties

Tumbled stones: smooth, versatile and affordable; perfect for beginners; ideal for keeping in a pocket.

Cluster crystals: bigger, heavier and very beautiful; they look as if they've been hewn from the rock.

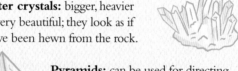

Pyramids: can be used for directing energies or positioned at the centre of an arrangement (or "grid").

Spheres: famously used as a focus for fortune-telling and internal meditation.

Cubes: grounding, solid and reliable.

Hearts: useful for emotions, romance, self-love and self-care.

Deciding on the ideal stone for a particular purpose is a bit like story-telling, connecting yourself to past traditions and ideas, while satisfying your own creative instincts. For example, if you want to make an incantation for romance, choose the heart-shaped rose quartz we talked about on page 52. If you'd like to make an affirmation that will get you through a difficult time at work, pick a cube (for stability and strength) of tiger's eye (for new perspectives on the problem, and to keep you grounded). And if you'd like to make a talisman for protection that you can keep in your pocket for tricky days ahead, select turquoise (an ancient stone of safety) that's been tumbled to make it smooth, so that it will feel satisfying in your hand when you reach for it.

EXERCISE:
Cleansing Your Crystals

Cleansing crystals is, essentially, a ritualized way to make them a "blank slate" for your thoughts, emotions and vibes. It's supposed to take away any negative energies that the stone might have absorbed on its way to you, so that you and the crystal can begin your journey together anew.

There are a number of ways to cleanse crystals, including smudging them with incense (see opposite), soaking them in salt water or bathing them in sunlight. It's always best to look up the right method for your crystal. Some crystals are too delicate for salt water and should just be lightly smudged with smoke; others will become cloudy if smudged and should just be left in direct sunlight, surrounded by a ring of table salt.

Properly cleansed, crystals can be used with a range of affirmations and incantations to create the reality you want: to clear your mind, to steady your resolve and to focus your ambitions and goals.

You will need: a crystal, an incense stick and a feather.

1 Place your crystal on a table in front of you. In one hand, take an incense stick and light it. In the other hand, take a feather. Using the feather and the stick together, waft the smoke over the crystal.

2 Take the crystal in your hands. Breathe in and out deeply, breathing in through the nose and out through the mouth.

3 Feel the weight of the crystal in your hands and your breath in your throat, the scent of incense still in the air. Be aware of yourself, and your surroundings.

4 Focus on the crystal in your hands. If you like, you could say "I clear this crystal of all past energies". However, you don't have to say anything; you might prefer simply to focus on your breath and the stone. Do whatever makes sense for you.

5 Ask yourself: What do I need reminding of? What do I want this talisman to be? What do I need? If you like, you

could say, for example, "I imbue this stone with strength and power". As before, you don't need to say anything; you might prefer to focus on imbuing the stone with your preferred energy.

What To Do With Your Crystals

Once your crystals are cleansed, you can use them to create talismans of your intentions. There are many ways to do this, and really it's up to each individual witch to work out what works for her. Here are some ideas:

- Write a list of your goals and keep the list under a crystal as a visual reminder of where you're hoping to go.

- Place a crystal on your bedside table to remind you to fall into better sleeping habits. (Some people believe that the stones can help soothe our subconsciousness for better sleep overall.)

- Make a crystal grid. Arranging your crystals in patterns and formations can be simultaneously creatively satisfying and immensely meditative.

- Keep a crystal on your desk to remind you that you're so much more than just your work, and to help you get through the day.

- Carry a crystal with you to act as a talismanic reminder of the person you're hoping to become.

The Future, Fortunes and Tarot

We all know about fortune-telling: you cross the palm of some withered old crone with silver, and she tells you that you will meet someone tall, dark and handsome.

It's nonsense, of course. In a world that's often profoundly chaotic, how can anyone tell what might happen next? Furthermore, in a world with free will, how can anyone hope to guess what *you* might *choose* to do next?

The thing about fortune-telling is that it can make us feel stuck. It can make us feel as though the future's already planned out for us; like we're just pawns in a cosmic game of chess. When considering fortune-telling, it's important to realize that we're talking about one of any number of possible futures – not what *will* be, but what *might* be. We're talking about options. We're talking about possibilities. We're talking about new perspectives.

As one famous wizard said to another: "It is our choices … that show what we truly are, far more than our abilities."[1]

Why Tarot?

There are a million methods of fortune-telling. Most cultures have some kind of ritual for predicting the future, whether it's reading the tea leaves left at the bottom of a cup or the movements of the stars. Any of these can work for you, if you know how to do them. In this book, however, we're focussing on Tarot.

We're going to talk about Tarot cards largely because they are really easy to use. You can choose a deck and start straightaway, kind of teaching yourself by looking stuff up. You can try different patterns, and you can make a reading as short or as long as you'd like.

Before we start, however, you need to forget everything you think you know about the Tarot. That "old lady with the headscarf and a pack of cards that says death" stereotype has very little to do with why you, right now, in the modern world, are thinking about using Tarot to help you.

What is Tarot?

There's a lot of mystique around Tarot. You might have heard that it's unlucky to buy your own pack of cards; or that you ought to keep them tied up in silk or velvet and sleep with them under your pillow; or that nobody should ever touch your cards but you.

Personally, I don't subscribe to most of it. I bought my cards for myself; I keep them in my handbag, tied with a spare hairband; and I don't mind anyone touching them if they ask. Tarot cards are a useful tool of the trade, that's all. Mine were printed in China and sold on a popular e-commerce site: the magic inherent in my cards comes from the artistry of the illustrator, the history of the symbols and the stories I tell myself when I use them.

Tarot works because it's a way to tell ourselves stories. It's a way to look at our lives and make them into a narrative that makes sense.

Choosing Your Deck

It might be a good idea to get hold of a deck of tarot cards before reading the rest of this chapter: it's easier to get the hang of something if you can play along at home.

You can get many kinds of Tarot deck with different illustrations and styles of illustration, but the meanings usually remain the same. The most famous Tarot deck for divination (or fortune-telling) is the Rider-Waite. First issued in 1910, this deck features coloured pen-and-ink drawings with a kind of traditional, medieval-esque feel to them. Lots of people love the Rider-Waite, taking solace in the idea that there is a hundred years of history behind them, but you may be drawn to a different deck.

I have everything from a cat-themed pop-culture pack to a set where each card features the image of a Byzantine saint. Personally, I mostly favour a "pip deck", which is a deck with minimal illustration.

What matters is that the deck feels right to you. Don't worry too much: the deck you're using now doesn't have to be your "forever" deck. It's just a good place to start. Some decks come with a helpful manual, which is a great way to get into Tarot.

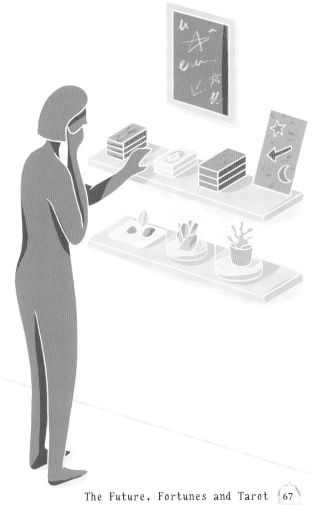

Understanding Tarot Cards

A Tarot deck is a set of illustrated cards that's a bit like a regular deck of playing cards. In fact, if you know what's what, you can actually tell Tarot with playing cards; it's just harder.

First made about five hundred years ago, Tarot cards are full of images and stories that can help you identify symbols and stories in your own life. Michelle Tea, a Tarot expert, says that Tarot is "an ancient story system, a pack of cards that tell a multitude of tales depending on the ways in which they're placed alongside one another"[2].

The Minor Arcana

There are four suits in a Tarot deck. They are generally called Cups, Wands, Swords and Pentacles. (They are, of course, also linked to the four elements: Cups to Water; wands to Fire; swords to Air; pentacles to Earth.) Each suit has ten cards, plus a King, a Queen, a Page (like the Jack) and a Knight. With me so far?

Each suit contains 14 cards, and together they form the minor arcana. These 56 cards represent most of what happens to us; they symbolize the majority of the feelings, events and ideas that make up our lives.

Each suit pertains to a different area of life:

Cups tend to deal with emotions and relationships.

Wands (also known as Rods) tend to be about passions.

Swords are the suit of the mind: they tend to be about strife.

Pentacles (also known as Coins) tend to deal with money and work.

The numbers on the minor arcana cards also mean something. As a general rule:

1 **Aces** are the purest essence of the suit. This is the dream of the suit – the dream of work or love or passion or thought.

2 **Twos** are hard work, although it's the positive kind of work.

3 **Threes** show you're getting somewhere: a solid, cheerful three.

4 **Fours** are pretty okay, although it's starting to get tricky.

5 **Fives** are mostly horrible: hard, glum horrible work.

6 **Sixes** are much better. Sixes show your work is paying off!

7 **Sevens** are hard again, but you've got your six behind you, and you know you can do it.

8 **Eights** are about looking at where you've come from, and where you're going.

9 **Nines** are my least favourites: something big is coming.

10 **Tens** are the end of the cycle: the big thing, whatever it was, has come. And now what?

The Major Arcana

The remaining 22 suitless cards in the Tarot deck are picture cards. We call them the major arcana, and they represent the big events in life, the big ideas and significant people, thoughts and places.

These cards are called (in order):

- The Magician
- The High Priestess
- The Empress
- The Emperor
- The Hierophant
- The Lovers
- The Chariot
- Strength
- The Hermit
- Wheel of Fortune
- Justice
- The Hanged Man
- Death
- Temperance
- The Devil
- The Tower
- The Star
- The Moon
- The Sun
- Judgment
- The World
- The Fool

Reading Tarot Cards

Each card of the major or minor arcana can represent you, or a person or situation. The same card can mean different things to different people, and often does. It's all about the stories we choose to tell, which is what makes Tarot such a powerful tool for divining the future.

Say, for example, you pull The Tower. This is a card about things toppling down; about past orders being destroyed. It might represent a relationship that's over, or a house move, or maybe something that you've been clinging onto that isn't

really healthy or helpful for you any more. It might represent a death, or it could represent the death of a way of life (such as, for example, if you've just had a baby).

Does this sound vague? It's supposed to. Is it magic? I couldn't possibly say. Certainly, I find that the cards I pull are often scarily apt, but the human mind is very

good at making
stories from nothing.
And it's the stories we're
really after here.

You've probably heard of
cold reading. It's the technique of
asking the right questions to find out
the most information. While it's often
seen as exploitative, all it really comes
down to (in a safe environment) is
tuning into the other person.

Tarot, just like all the witchcraft in
this book, is simply an exercise in
using the trappings of magic to help
you understand the story of your life.

EXERCISE:
Preparing Your Cards

This is how I always begin a reading, although there are lots of ways to do it.

You will need: a candle and your Tarot deck.

1 Light a candle and remove your deck from its wrappings.

2 Shuffle the deck the way you'd normally shuffle a regular deck of playing cards, then cut it.

3 Put the deck back together any way you like. Shuffle the deck again, then cut the deck into three, as evenly or unevenly as you like.

4 Put each third of the deck, face-down, on the table, then put the deck back together any way you like and shuffle once more.

5 Put the deck, face-down, on the table and, using the side and flat of your hand, fan the cards out.

You are now ready to use your Tarot cards. On the following pages, you'll find an exercise designed to help you get to know the cards and a guide to the three-card spread.

EXERCISE:
Getting To Know Your Cards

The process of getting to know your cards can take a while.
To work through the whole deck would take a day or more,
so plan to spend about an hour on this the first time you do it,
then repeat the process as many times as you need, until you
know all the cards like old friends.

You will need: a candle and your Tarot deck.

1 Light a candle and prepare the cards by following steps
   1–5 on the previous page.

2 Pull a card at random. For now, we're just getting to know
   the cards, not trying to tell a fortune. Using the information
   on pages 68–71 and the picture on the card, too, guess what
   you think the card might mean.

3 Then, using either online resources or a book about Tarot,
   look up another interpretation. Maybe look up a few
   interpretations to give you an idea of nuance. Think of a
   person you know who embodies the spirit of the card. Is
   there a place or maybe a time in your life when this card
   might have been relevant?

4 Focus on the candle flame, then transfer that focus to the image on the card. Fix that card, together with your impressions of the card, in your mind.

5 Return the card to the deck and repeat steps 2–4 for as long as you'd like.

EXERCISE:
The Three-card Spread

The simplest kind of reading is a three-card spread. I like to light a candle for ambience but it's not essential – I've done this reading on a bus, in a queue at the supermarket and even on a beach.

You will need: a candle (optional) and your Tarot deck.

1 Light a candle, if using, and prepare the cards by following steps 1–5 of Preparing Your Cards (page 74).

2 Focus your mind on a question. Draw three cards. The first card represents your past, the second card represents your present and the third card represents your future.

3 Now, remember, Tarot only tells us what we already know. We use the cards to prompt a story of what *might* be, and to create a narrative of what's gone before. For example, perhaps we need to be more High Priestess at work or more Six-of-Rods about our own achievements. Perhaps The Tower needs to come down. Perhaps we're being Five-of-Cups about something we should have left in the past. Tarot gives us new perspectives on our present and past, and simply an idea of what the future might be.

Making Something From Nothing

There's something special about creating things. I know a witch who knits her wishes for people into each row of her socks and scarves. I dig in my garden and plant my hopes for my life down deep with the basil and parsley. The act of bringing something out of almost nothing (or disparate ingredients) always feels like a blessing, whether it is or not. The ordinary acts of writing, cooking or building a house are the kind of everyday magic that everyone can aspire toward.

Making your own tools for witchcraft can be akin to a spell in itself: a double spell, once in the making and once in the casting. In this chapter, we'll look at two small acts of creation: candle-making (and a brief meditation to go along with it) and a little window-box to act as a witch's kitchen garden (along with advice on the properties of various herbs).

The Power of Fire

We have honoured three of the four physical elements in our practice so far: using crystals (Earth), smudging with smoke (Air) and reading Tarot, which could be said to have a fluid narrative (Water). The final physical element, then, is one we've touched on in every ritual and affirmation in this book: the element of Fire.

Much of modern witchcraft asks us to begin by lighting a candle. This is, perhaps, because focussing on a candle flame is profoundly hypnotic, making it easier to enter the semi-trancelike meditative state we need to focus our energies in a concentrated fashion. It also lowers the heart rate, pulse and blood pressure, which means that it's good for us both mentally and physically, whether we believe in magic or not.

There's another reason why so many spells begin with the lighting of a candle. It's because the transfiguration of wax to light to smoke to air is the simplest way of showing that matter and energy can move from one state to another. It shows us that nothing is permanent; that to be alive is to be in a state of flux.

The relationship between what we are and what we do is so complex that, even scientifically speaking, it's hard to separate physics from magic. This is perhaps why we're so drawn to firelight: it's at once profoundly simple and infinitely complex. Just like us.

Candle-making

You will need: beeswax, a heatproof bowl, a saucepan, a stirrer, a wick, a jar and an essential oil that matches your intention for the candle (see pages 84–87).

1 Break the beeswax into a heatproof bowl set over a saucepan of boiling water, making sure that the bottom of the bowl doesn't touch the water. Stir gently, focussing your mind on the melting wax and concentrating only on the movement of your stirrer and the way the wax is melting. (This is a good time to visualize any bad feelings dissipating and turning back into energy.) This process should take about 15 minutes.

2 Affix the wick to the base of the jar. (If you like, you can dip the end of the wick in the melted wax, to act as a further security.)

3 Add seven drops of the essential oil to the melted beeswax, saying, "I make this candle for [focus, or love, or calm, or whatever]." Stir seven times clockwise.

4 Add seven more drops of the essential oil, and stir seven times anticlockwise, repeating the statement out loud.

5 Carefully pour the scented wax into the prepared jar, holding the wick upright. (You may find it easiest to tie the wick to a lollipop stick resting on the rim of the jar.) Let cool.

When you use this candle for incantations and affirmations, remember that you made the candle, and now you turn it into purest light.

The Witch's Kitchen Garden

Many ancient branches of witchcraft hinge on kitchen gardens. Furthermore, many historic witches were branded as such because of their knowledge of powerful herbs that acted as medicines, stimulants or depressants. In the modern world, most of us are lucky enough to have access to medicines, but there's no reason why we shouldn't also carry on the tradition of making something from nothing by growing and using herbs.

There's something amazing about sinking your hands into the dirt and watching plants grow, even if you live in a studio in the city. Gardening has been proven to lift mood, help depression and insomnia, and to improve overall physical health. Plus, the meditative effects of carefully nurturing and tending to a garden can make a huge difference to mental health – and what's that if not magic?

To assemble a little garden, you will need a suitable trough, some potting compost and a few plants. For beginners, the easiest way to start your garden is with pots of supermarket herbs, which, if tended carefully, can flourish.

The Properties (Magical and Otherwise) of Herbs

Rosemary: associated for centuries with memory, rosemary has been scientifically proven to improve concentration and focus. Plus, it will grow outside very happily and flowers beautifully, even in winter.

Lemon balm: this herb is said to restore lost youth. It also makes a beautiful, soothing tea with mint that aids digestion.

Basil (especially holy basil): in Ayurvedic medicine, basil promotes clarity and focus. It's said to reduce stress and encourage prosperity. (It's also great with spaghetti – there's nothing more magical than supper!)

Lavender: this plant is scientifically shown to help us to relax; to improve sleep quality, elevate moods and even – in some cases – to help alleviate pain. It is reasonably hardy and can be grown outside.

Bay: as well as being beautiful and glossy-leaved, bay trees are a symbol of protection. Laurel (its other name) has been used for celebration and triumph since at least the time of the ancient Greeks. Why not grow your own miniature bay tree to bring these qualities into your home?

Sage: this is the ultimate cleansing herb. Dried and smoked sage is used in Native American tradition to drive out evil and to begin anew.

If you can't grow your own herbs, essential oils will allow you to get some of the same benefits.

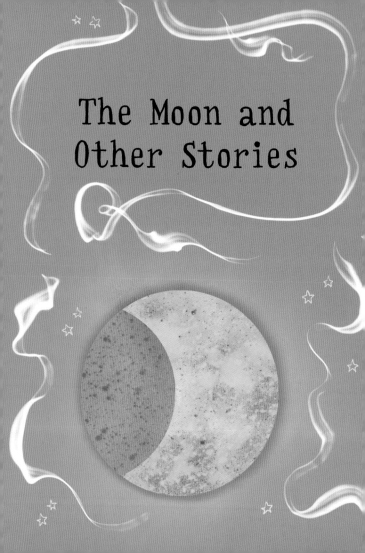

The Moon and
Other Stories

Moonlight is magical: think of a great yellow harvest moon or the strange power of a rare blue moon or the thin silver sickle of the moon before it almost seems to disappear. Even for the non-witchily inclined, it's hard to resist the pull of the moon.

The moon has a very special place in witchcraft. Traditionally, witches practised under the moon; were governed (as most women are) by its waxing and waning 28-day cycle; and lived their lives by its light.

Being in touch with the moon allows us to be in touch with ourselves: to think of where we were last full moon or the moon before; and to think of what's changed in our lives since then. It allows us to find ourselves in time – the way that staring up into the night sky allows us to find our place in space.

EXERCISE:
Keeping a Moon Journal

Every night for a month, make a concerted effort to keep a moon journal.

You will need: a journal and a pen.

1 Go outside and look at the moon. Allow yourself four or five minutes to really study it.

2 Write down your impressions in the journal. If it's cloudy, describe the clouds; if it's pitch-black, describe the darkness. You're looking to create a record of what it was to be alive on this particular night – to make a note of who you were and who the moon was at that moment. The notes don't have to be long, but they should be as vivid as you can make them. What colour was the moon? What shape? Was it high or low in the sky? Were there stars? Where were you?

The Universe

So much of magic is
about accepting our
place in the
universe. It's about
really seeing who
we are, where we are
and what we can do.
It's about thinking hard
about all our options, whether
that's reading Tarot to give us an idea
of our own story; or planting a garden to prove that we have
the power to create; or focussing on a crystal to remember
that we made a resolution to do something, or be something,
or change something.

And yet, when we look at the night sky, we see that all of
this is almost nothing. In the grand scheme of things, we're
nothing; and yet here we are, with whole worlds inside us.
And that's the magic of the thing.

This might seem a frightening concept, but to me, it's
comforting. So much of magic is about accepting that there
are forces in the universe we can't understand.

There isn't room in this book to get into astrology: it's vastly complicated, and there's no way to simplify it without losing something vital in the telling. Nonetheless, to observe the stars is to know that our own sun is one of those stars. We're all moving through an unknowable universe that is itself, perhaps, moving through many other universes. There is so much that we don't know.

Observing the night sky lets us see that we're part of something bigger than our comprehension. Magic can give us this, too.

Conclusion

This book has been a very brief introduction to witchcraft and magic. We've touched on many subjects about which whole books have been written. There are almost certainly places in the book where witches who are more experienced than me will have sucked their teeth and wondered what I'm talking about – there are always more experienced witches; there are always people to learn from. That's part of the joy of this journey, and the reason I've written this book.

Witchcraft is having a cultural "moment", true. But then, maybe witchcraft has always been having a moment. As long as there have been women who wanted to think for themselves and control their own lives, there have been women who were called witches.

The idea of the witch is the idea of the independent woman: a woman who understands herself and the world around her, and acts on that understanding to make things happen. And it's so much more than that. It's women with enough self-worth to believe they can make things happen. It's women with enough humility to admit there are always forces in the universe we don't understand. It's women with enough imagination, curiosity and strength to try something different. It's women learning from other women. It's women unlocking their own power. It's powerful, radical magic that's yours for the taking. That's what all of this book has been about.

Endnotes

1 Rowling, JK. *Harry Potter and the Chamber of Secrets* (Bloomsbury Children's Books, London, 2014).

2 Tea, Michelle. *Modern Tarot: Connecting with Your Higher Self through the Wisdom of the Cards* (HarperOne, London, 2017).

Acknowledgements

I would like to thank my coven – in particular Noelle, Elizabeth and Blue – for their dedicated help and support with this book.

I would also like to thank the numerous historians, sociologists, archaeologists and academics whose work has been invaluable to me over the years in increasing my understanding of this ancient art.

I would also like to thank Tarot scholar Caroline O'Donoghue for her kind interest in this project from the very beginning: this book would be very different without her willing and expert eye.